BAGHDAD PUPS

by Meish Goldish

Consultant: Terri Crisp
Program Manager, Operation Baghdad Pups
SPCA International
New York, New York

PUBLISHING

New York, New York

Credits

Cover and Title Page, © Courtesy of Luke Henry; Cover TR, Courtesy of Terri Crisp/SPCA International; Cover CR, Courtesy of Terri Crisp/SPCA International; Cover BR, Courtesy of Terri Crisp/SPCA International; TOC, Courtesy of Dave Alvarez; 4, Courtesy of Edward Watson; 5, Courtesy of Edward Watson; 6, Courtesy of Edward Watson; 7, Courtesy of Edward Watson; 8, © AP Images/Mike Derer; 9, © Carol Guzy/The Washington Post/Getty Images; 10, © AP Images/Mike Derer; 11, Courtesy of Terri Crisp/SPCA International; 12, © U.S. Marine Corps photo by Lance Cpl. Thomas Lew; 13, © AP Images/Lucy Pemoni; 14, Courtesy of Terri Crisp/SPCA International; 15, Courtesy of Terri Crisp/SPCA International; 16, Courtesy of Jeremy Kagan; 17, Courtesy of Jeremy Kagan; 18T, Courtesy of Dave Alvarez; 18B, Courtesy of Dave Alvarez; 19B, Courtesy of Dave Alvarez; 20, Courtesy of Dave Alvarez; 21, Courtesy of Dave Alvarez; 22, Courtesy of VetDogs; 23, Courtesy of Luke Henry; 24, © AP Images/Jacquelyn Martin; 25, © David Joles/Minneapolis Star Tribune/ZUMA Press; 26, Courtesy of Terri Crisp/SPCA International; 27, © David Joles/Minneapolis Star Tribune/ZUMA Press; 29T, © Eric Isselée/Shutterstock; 29B, © J. McPhail /Shutterstock.

Publisher: Kenn Goin
Senior Editor: Lisa Wiseman
Creative Director: Spencer Brinker
Design: Dawn Beard Creative
Photo Researcher: Amy Dunleavy

Library of Congress Cataloging-in-Publication Data

Goldish, Meish.
   Baghdad pups / by Meish Goldish.
     p. cm. — (Dog heroes)
   Includes bibliographical references and index.
   ISBN-13: 978-1-61772-150-2 (library binding)
   ISBN-10: 1-61772-150-6 (library binding)
   1. Dog rescue—Iraq—Baghdad—Anecdotes—Juvenile literature. 2. Dogs—Iraq—Baghdad—Anecdotes—Juvenile literature. 3. Dogs—Therapeutic use—Iraq—Baghdad—Juvenile literature. 4. United States—Armed Forces—Military life—Anecdotes—Juvenile literature. 5. Iraq War, 2003—Personal narratives, American—Juvenile literature. I. Title.
   HV4746.G65 2011
   956.7044'31—dc22
                        2010035187

For more information, write to Bearport Publishing Company, Inc., 101 Fifth Avenue, Suite 6R, New York, New York 10003. Printed in the United States of America in North Mankato, Minnesota.

121510
10810CGB

10 9 8 7 6 5 4 3 2 1

Winchester Public Library
Winchester, MA 01890
781-721-7171
www.winpublib.org

Table of Contents

A Wartime Secret

In 2007, U.S. Army **Sergeant** (Sgt.) Edward Watson was serving in the war in Iraq, a country in southwest Asia. One day, his **regiment** went on patrol in a dangerous neighborhood outside the city of Baghdad (BAG-dad). Suddenly, the soldiers spotted a tiny dog in the street. The black-and-white puppy was covered with fleas and weak from hunger. A soldier scooped him up and wrapped him in a blanket.

Sgt. Edward Watson and the puppy that he and the other soldiers found in Iraq

Upon returning to their **base**, Sergeant Watson and the other soldiers took turns secretly caring for their new buddy that they named Charlie. While they knew it was against U.S. **military** rules for soldiers to keep animals as pets, the tiny pup helped lift the men's spirits.

Charlie was as small as a potato when he was found as a puppy. He grew quickly, though. Here, he's shown playing with toys the soldiers gave him.

Most dogs in Iraq are **strays**. They live on the streets, often in **packs** of about 35 animals. Many Iraqi strays die from gunshot wounds, disease, beatings, or hunger. Most live for only a few years.

5

No Buddy Left Behind

As the soldiers spent time with Charlie, the bond between them grew even stronger. However, a problem soon arose. The group was scheduled to leave Iraq. Sergeant Watson feared that Charlie would die if he was left behind on the war-torn streets of Baghdad. He wanted to bring the dog home with him to America. However, military rules didn't allow it.

Once Charlie grew bigger, he often went on patrol with Sergeant Watson's regiment in Iraq.

Sergeant Watson decided to contact the Society for the Prevention of Cruelty to Animals International (SPCAI), a group that works to improve the safety and well-being of animals around the world. He thought that maybe they could help. Sergeant Watson told them, "I just can't leave our buddy behind."

SPCAI employees were touched by Sergeant Watson's request. After months of planning, they were able to fly Charlie out of Baghdad. In February 2008, he arrived in the United States to live with Sergeant Watson in Arizona.

It is against U.S. military rules to remove property, including animals, from a war zone. The rule is meant to show respect to the people of the country where the property or animal is found.

Today, Charlie enjoys a safe, healthy life in Arizona with Sergeant Watson and his family.

A Cause Is Born

Terri Crisp works for the SPCAI. When Sergeant Watson asked to keep his dog, she thought it would be the only request of its kind. She was wrong, however. In the coming months, more U.S. soldiers asked the SPCAI to help bring home dogs they had **befriended** in Iraq.

Terri Crisp (right) is an animal expert who works to save animals from dangerous situations such as wars, floods, fires, and earthquakes.

Terri agreed to help. In November 2007, she developed a new SPCAI program called Operation Baghdad Pups. Since then, the group has flown more than 200 dogs from Iraq to the United States.

"You're not only helping animals, you're helping our soldiers, too," Terri explained. "What better way can we say thank you?"

Terri hugs Charlie after bringing him back from Iraq.

Operation Baghdad Pups rescues cats as well as dogs. Since 2008, about 50 cats have been flown to the United States to live with American soldiers who returned home from Iraq.

9

A Deadly Surprise

Operation Baghdad Pups has been active for several years. Yet the U.S. military doesn't approve of the program. Why? One reason is that it breaks the military's rule against removing property from a war zone.

Though the military doesn't approve of the program, Operation Baghdad Pups continues to rescue dogs from Iraq.

The second reason is that the military is concerned about health risks after an incident in 2008. In June of that year, the SPCAI flew 24 dogs and 2 cats from Baghdad to the United States. Three days later, one of the dogs—a black Labrador (Lab) mix named Crusader—became very sick. He had to be **euthanized**. No one realized at the time that the dog had **rabies**. Would the other animals that had been on the flight get sick as well?

Crusader, an 11-month-old Iraqi dog, had to be euthanized after becoming seriously ill from rabies.

Rabies is a dangerous and sometimes deadly disease that can easily be spread from dogs to people and other animals, including other dogs, through dog bites.

Safety Measures

By the time Crusader's rabies was discovered, some of the other animals from the flight had already been flown to families across the United States. As a safety measure, health officials monitored all the pets. They were **vaccinated** and, in some cases, **quarantined** for six months to make sure they weren't sick as well.

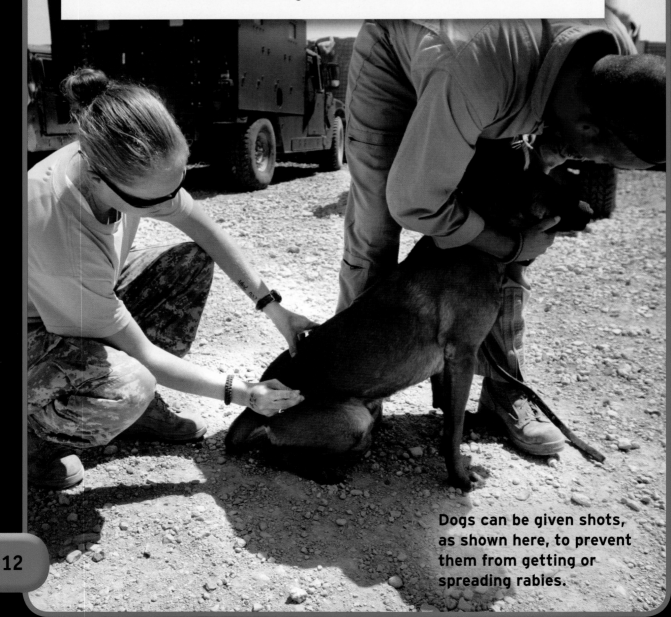

Dogs can be given shots, as shown here, to prevent them from getting or spreading rabies.

Luckily, no people or other animals got rabies from Crusader. Yet military officials worried that future Iraqi animals brought to America could create new health risks. So to prevent the spread of diseases by animals, the SPCAI now has all Iraqi dogs and cats vaccinated before traveling to America. If an animal is not vaccinated at least 30 days before leaving Iraq, it must be quarantined in America until the 30 days have passed.

A dog being quarantined

Rescued Iraqi dogs are usually healthy because most of them are mixed breeds, which are animals whose parents are two different types of dog. Mixed breeds are known to be stronger than purebreds, which are animals whose parents are the same type of dog.

Easing the Pain

Although they object to the efforts of Operation Baghdad Pups, the military has never tried to shut it down. Terri Crisp says, "I think a lot of officers recognize how important many of these dogs are to our soldiers."

One good example of their importance is a scrappy dog named Moody. American soldiers in Iraq found the little pup on a day when five members of their **company** were killed by a bomb.

Moody, shown here sleeping, helped the soldiers cope after they lost five fellow fighters in Iraq.

Moody proved to be a great comfort to the men. The soldiers hugged him and even felt comfortable enough to talk to him about their difficult loss. The dog gave them a chance to let out their emotions.

The company leader, Staff Sgt. Bryan Spears, said, "I think that if Moody had not been around, there would have been a lot of lost souls in the company." He added, "We didn't save Moody. Moody saved us."

Moody was part of the SPCAI's seventh rescue flight out of Iraq. He came to America in June 2008 to live with Sergeant Spears.

Sergeant Spears, Moody, and Terri Crisp

Team Effort

Dogs like Moody comfort soldiers at war. In return, the soldiers help the animals as much as possible. Phoenix is a puppy that a U.S. soldier in Iraq found in a pile of trash in 2008. The soldier and the other men in his **unit** took care of the pup. At first, they fed him scraps from their own meals. Then news of the dog spread to the soldiers' families and friends back in America. Soon, these caring people were sending dog food and toys to Phoenix.

Even though the soldiers didn't have much food for themselves, they made sure that Phoenix always had something to eat.

Phoenix was great company for the soldiers. They treated him like a family pet. When it came time for the unit to leave Iraq, the SPCAI flew Phoenix to America. He was going to live with one of the soldiers and his family, along with their other pets, which included five dogs, two cats, three horses, and a parrot!

Phoenix was flown to America in November 2009. He was part of the SPCAI's 39th rescue flight mission.

Phoenix rode with the soldiers while they were on patrol. Often, the dog sensed danger before the soldiers did.

Dogs on Duty

For American soldiers, stray dogs in Iraq can be more than just pets. In 2007, Petey and Penny were born on a U.S. military base near Baghdad. They grew up on the base, protecting the **Marines** there by barking at anyone they didn't know. Because the dogs were able to help guard the base, the military **classified** them as Force Protection **Canines**. Such dogs don't need to be kept a secret.

Petey (top) and Penny (bottom) on patrol in Iraq

Petey (left) and Penny (right) when they were puppies

One night in 2009, Petey and Penny left the base and they were shot. No one knows why they left or who shot them. Even though she lost a lot of blood, Penny managed to crawl one mile (1.6 km) back to base. A Marine named Dave Alvarez found the injured dog and rushed her to military doctors, who cleaned and stitched her wound. Yet where was Petey? Dave needed to find him—and fast!

Penny was treated for her face wound by doctors at the base and later was flown by helicopter to an animal clinic for surgery.

A Force Protection Canine receives **benefits** from the military, such as being allowed to be treated by a veterinarian.

Sad and Glad

Dave set out on a desperate search for Petey. He followed Penny's long trail of blood, which led him to Petey's dead body. Dave and the other Marines at the base were very sad and upset when they learned that Petey had been killed. Yet their spirits were boosted three weeks later when Penny returned from the clinic. After several surgeries, her wounds had finally healed.

Dave grew close to Penny while serving at the Marine base.

Later, Dave asked the SPCAI to fly Penny to his family's home in Arizona. "Penny is one tough cookie," he told them. "She lost a ton of blood that day, and it's a miracle she is alive. She's done her job very well for years and she does not deserve to be left behind."

The SPCAI agreed. With the help of their rescue team, they managed to get Penny out of Iraq.

In January 2010, the SPCAI flew Penny to Arizona to live with Dave and his family.

Penny poses with Dave's wife, Holly.

A Daring Rescue

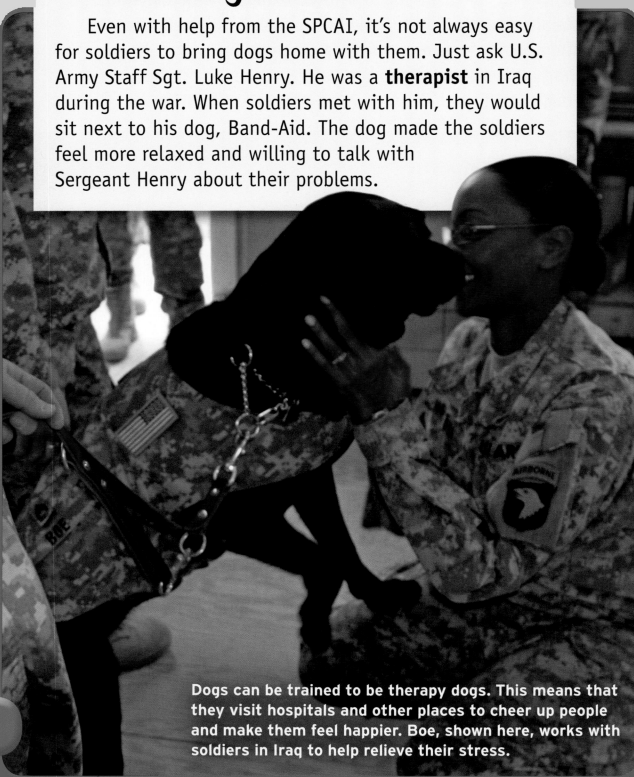

Even with help from the SPCAI, it's not always easy for soldiers to bring dogs home with them. Just ask U.S. Army Staff Sgt. Luke Henry. He was a **therapist** in Iraq during the war. When soldiers met with him, they would sit next to his dog, Band-Aid. The dog made the soldiers feel more relaxed and willing to talk with Sergeant Henry about their problems.

Dogs can be trained to be therapy dogs. This means that they visit hospitals and other places to cheer up people and make them feel happier. Boe, shown here, works with soldiers in Iraq to help relieve their stress.

When Sergeant Henry was due to leave Iraq, he arranged for the SPCAI to fly Band-Aid to America. However, an army veterinarian found out about the plan and tried to stop them. So, Sergeant Henry hid with the dog overnight in an empty shack. In the morning, he left Band-Aid with a stranger who promised to get the dog to the SPCAI. Luckily, she kept her word. In December 2008, Sergeant Henry and Band-Aid were **reunited** in America.

Staff Sgt. Luke Henry with Band-Aid

"It was the scariest thing I think I have ever done," Sergeant Henry said of his effort to save Band-Aid. "When I handed my dog to the woman who said she would help, I didn't know if I would ever see Band-Aid again."

Power of the People

It took one stranger's help to rescue Band-Aid from Iraq. For Ratchet, however, it took 70,000 strangers! Ratchet was a puppy that U.S. Army Sgt. Gwen Beberg had saved from a pile of burning trash. When her duty in Iraq ended, the army told Sergeant Beberg that she had to leave Ratchet behind.

Sergeant Beberg begged the SPCAI for help. "Ratchet is everything to me!" she wrote to them. "I couldn't have made it through this **deployment** without his wagging tail and understanding eyes."

Ratchet

The SPCAI tried to convince army officials to change their minds about Ratchet. However, they refused. So a friend of Sergeant Beberg put a **petition** on the Internet asking the army to allow her to keep the dog. More than 70,000 people signed the petition. The effort paid off. In October 2008, the dog was flown to Minnesota to rejoin the Sergeant.

Ratchet and Sergeant Beberg happily reunite in the United States.

The army stopped the SPCAI twice from rescuing Ratchet before finally allowing the dog to be flown to America.

The Work Goes On

Today, Operation Baghdad Pups continues to rescue dogs from Iraq. Up to 103 animals have been flown to America each year since 2008. Every rescue requires careful planning. SPCAI workers must first hire a U.S. security team to pick up the dogs and drive them to the Baghdad airport. Then SPCAI workers must travel to the airport in Baghdad so that they can fly back with the dogs to America.

American SPCAI workers, such as Bev Westerman (left) and Terri Crisp (right), travel to Baghdad International Airport in order to fly back to the United States with the rescued dogs.

The struggle to save these dogs is not easy—or cheap. It costs about $4,000 to rescue each animal. The money pays for the security team, plus airfares and overnight hotel rooms for SPCAI workers. It also pays for the dog's medical expenses, including vaccinations. Although it is costly, Operation Baghdad Pups continues its hard work so that "no buddy will be left behind."

Dogs rescued by the SPCAI live safe and healthy lives in America.

Each Iraqi dog rescue is paid for entirely through donations. The SPCAI asks the soldier's family to donate $1,000. However, it never refuses to rescue a dog because the family cannot afford to pay.

27

Just the Facts

- The SPCAI does not rescue just any dog from Iraq. A rescued dog must have been originally found as a puppy under the age of three months. The dog also must be in good health, well behaved, and never have bitten a person.

- Each Iraqi dog must be in U.S. military care for at least two months before it can come to America. A dog found by soldiers just a few weeks before they leave Iraq will not be rescued.

- Before a dog can leave Iraq, the soldier who found the dog or a family member must be willing to give the pet a home. The dog cannot be sent to an animal shelter to be adopted.

- The SPCAI has rescued two dogs for American soldiers fighting in Afghanistan, a country in southwest Asia. It's harder to rescue dogs in Afghanistan than in Iraq. Why? It's very difficult for Afghan drivers who are carrying dogs in their vehicles to get across the country without being shot at. Enemy forces always assume the drivers are helping American soldiers stationed there.

Common Breeds: BAGHDAD PUPS

Most of the dogs that are rescued by Operation Baghdad Pups are mixed breeds. Here are two of the most common types.

Border-collie mix

Labrador mix

base (BAYSS) the place where soldiers live or operate from

befriended (bi-FREND-id) made friends with someone

benefits (BEN-uh-fits) help in the form of money or services given to a member of a group

canines (KAY-nyenz) members of the dog family

classified (KLASS-uh-fide) put into a particular group based on ability or characteristics

company (KUHM-puh-nee) a group of soldiers serving under the same captain

deployment (di-PLOI-muhnt) the placement of soldiers in one or more areas

euthanized (YOO-thuh-nized) a humane method for ending the life of an animal that's suffering

Marines (muh-REENZ) members of the U.S. Marine Corps who are trained to fight on land and at sea

military (MIL-uh-*ter*-ee) having to do with soldiers and the armed forces

packs (PAKS) groups of animals that live and travel together

petition (puh-TISH-uhn) a letter signed by many people asking those in power to change their rules or actions

quarantined (KWOR-uhn-teend) separated from others in order to stop a disease from spreading

rabies (RAY-beez) an often deadly disease spread by the bite of an infected animal that can affect humans, dogs, bats, and other warm-blooded animals

regiment (REJ-uh-muhnt) a large group of soldiers made up of two or more military units

reunited (*ree*-yoo-NITE-id) joined or brought together again

sergeant (SAR-juhnt) an officer in the U.S. Army or Marines who is in charge of the troops

strays (STRAYZ) dogs or cats that are lost or don't have homes

therapist (THER-uh-pist) a person who is trained to treat patients for emotional problems

unit (YOO-nit) a group or division in the armed forces that is part of a larger group or division

vaccinated (VAK-suh-*nayt*-id) given a medicine that helps protect against disease

Bibliography

George, Isabel. *The Dog That Saved My Life: Incredible True Stories of Canine Loyalty Beyond All Bounds.* New York: HarperElement (2010).

Kopelman, Jay, with Melinda Roth. *From Baghdad with Love: A Marine, the War, and a Dog Named Lava.* Guilford, CT: Lyons Press (2008).

Sullivan, Christine. *Saving Cinnamon: The Amazing True Story of a Missing Military Puppy and the Desperate Mission to Bring Her Home.* New York: St. Martin's Press (2009).

Swan, Madeline. *Dogs at War: Canine Heroes of Outstanding Courage and Bravery.* London: Max Press (2010).

Read More

Apte, Sunita. *Combat-Wounded Dogs.* New York: Bearport (2010).

Halls, Kelly Milner, and Major William Sumner. *Saving the Baghdad Zoo: A True Story of Hope and Heroes.* New York: Greenwillow (2010).

Ruffin, Frances E. *Military Dogs.* New York: Bearport (2007).

Learn More Online

Visit these Web sites to learn more about Operation Baghdad Pups:

www.petside.com/the-sidewalk/operation-baghdad-pups.php

www.SPCAI.org/baghdad-pups.html

www.wusa9.com/rss/local_article.aspx?storyid=68560%20

Index

About the Author

Meish Goldish has written more than 200 books for children. His books *Bug-a-licious* and *Michael Phelps: Anything Is Possible* were Children's Choices Reading List Selections in 2010. He lives in Brooklyn, New York.